PERENNIAL

Perennial

T. TONEY

I. D.

T. Toney

For you:
Thank you for holding my hand along this journey.

To the constant sources of my inspiration:
Thank you for letting me immortalize you in my work.

Illustrations done by: I. D.
Thank you for taking the time out of your busy schedule to help me.

Contents

Dedication iv

SELF

PLATONIC 65

ROMANTIC 84

SOMEWHERE IN THE MIDDLE 121

Self

Honesty

This order of love is important –
how can you love others
if you simply can't love yourself?

What makes it so hard for you
to treat yourself
how you treat everyone else?
The ones you love,
the ones you respect,
the ones you understand.

Extend yourself
the same courtesy you extend others.

Language

"No" is a dead language.
"No" jumped over foreign
when I was assaulted for the first time at eighteen,
voice hoarse from pleading
and
my breasts hurt as much as my legs –
I remember what it felt like
to want to blush in embarrassment
when trying to sit and a yelp left my lips.

Why was I more embarrassed than angry that "No"
wasn't the proverbial stop sign that was promised –
and
there was "No" ticket for the speeding past it –
"No" court date for the body used as a speed bump –
"No" consequences for anyone but me,
me left with gravel in my mouth
weighing down the screams
that threatened to pull me apart,
crumpled up in the ditch
society labeled 'asking for it."
Me left with the knowledge that

"No" never had any power in the first place.

So "No" became a dead language
fortified by the confusion that rippled
over the face of my then husband when I said it –
shrugged off as I was backed into a wall
and
decisions were laid out in front of me
and
in his anger
"No" going liquid and dripping from my mouth
like drool or blood,
I could "No" longer tell.

"No" was an omen used against nonbelievers
"No" was a broken barrier still advertised as whole
"No" is now a safety net with a hole in the middle
and
we're jumping from the fiftieth floor,
"No" was that ran over stop sign from my childhood –
tacked to the wall for a laugh over how it was stolen.

"No" became a dead language
and
my mouth it's graveyard
tombstone erected dead center
on my tongue
and
scraping against the roof of my mouth
titled "Why?"
so, I tripped over it,
or was it so I don't forget to use it?

"No" was enough of a reason
and
I know that now.

"No" loses it's meaning the second it's ignored
and
while Latin will welcome it over
I refuse to allow "No" to become a dead language,
but society is great at making dead languages
by telling its people:
'She must not have meant it,'
because "No" isn't supposed to be
a catch all dish by the door,
where I place the keys to my bodily autonomy
and
trust you not to make a spare,
to not crack me wide open
and
make yourself at home:
the intrusion feels like a house on fire,
the arsonist long gone
and
the tire tracks in the yard washed away
by apathy,
while I realize "No" is officially a dead language.

Self-Hatred

I still feel the bruises
on my breasts
where your mouth assaulted my flesh:
rough and painful –
painful, painful, painful,

pleasure
My thighs clench together.
I hate this feeling.
I hate you.
I hate myself most of all.

Sing For Me

A different set of hands on my hips,
A new presence in my temple:
Daily, weekly, monthly.
I felt nothing.

A song of self-destruction

Everything Unspoken

My body starts to crumble
decay –
A hollowed-out crevice forming
then sinking in on itself
the smell unmistakable.
Bloated feelings
and
maggot covered clots:
the putrid smell of
thoughts left to rot,
left unburied
in the chasm my self-worth fled from.

Never Enough

I found myself looking for "love"
within the arms of strangers
and
hoping they could fill the hole in my heart
the same way they filled my pussy:

full to bursting
and
with extreme enthusiasm

but all I got were sticky thighs
and
goosebumps.
It took me keeping my legs closed
to realize
that I wasn't looking for "love",
I was looking for validation.

Pigment

What I wouldn't do
to change skins with you.
You could be black
and I,
oh, I could be whatever I wanted.
oh, I could do whatever I wanted.

Identity

an entity,
so unsure if they wish to be perceived
or not –
so unsure of what being in this skin entails.
Just trying to find a way
to be comfortable.
just trying to find a way
to be me.

Casual Murder

I'll assemble a tombstone
for these feelings,
as soon as I process
exactly why I killed them
in the first place.

Roadkill

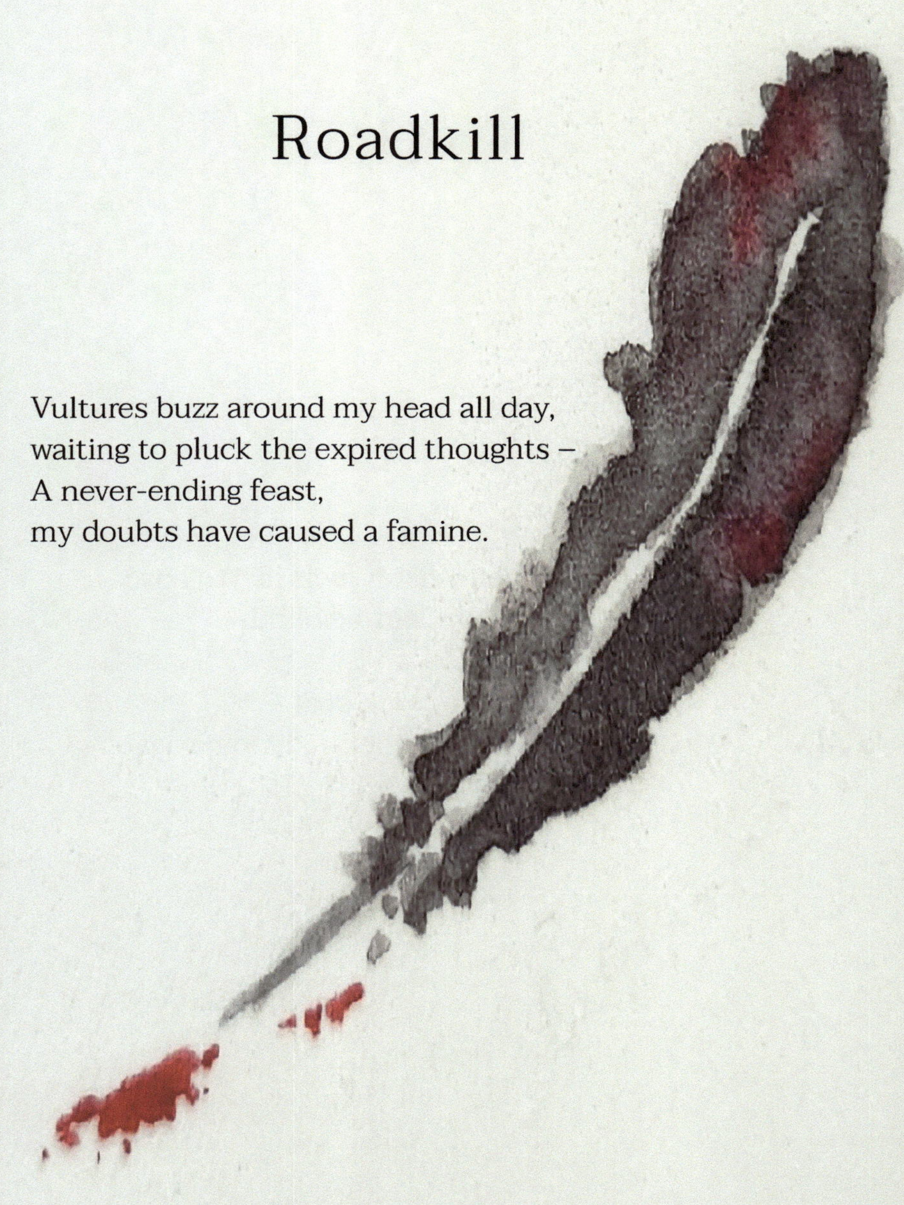

Vultures buzz around my head all day,
waiting to pluck the expired thoughts –
A never-ending feast,
my doubts have caused a famine.

No Help

I can tell you what it feels like to have:
your heart be blind
and
your brain deaf –
leaving the rest of your body to navigate.

Balancing Act

I sometimes feel too much
or
too little –
is there ever perfect balance?
No:
you're always going to be at war with yourself.
In a constant argument with what you want
and
what you need.
There is no such thing as perfect balance,
you can only balance to the best of your ability.

Face First

Here I am again:

stumbling,

tripping,

falling

right back into my bad habits.
With my eyes wide open,
I anticipate the crash
but can never handle the pain that follows.
Why is it so hard
to stop doing
the things that hurt me?

Release

Why is it so hard to let go
of things that no longer serve me?
Is it because I'll miss the comfort that familiarity brings
or
am I scared that I'll never love something else the same?

Heathen

I wish I could use religion like a band aid –
slap it against everything that pains me
and
let it keep out all the dirt,
but sadly
I could never feel God's light,
even when I tried.
I prayed,
I begged,
I pleaded,
until finally I decided to do nothing,
Yet religion never was meant to be a band aid for me:
I had to constantly patch my own self up
and
there's only so much 'hope'
I managed to hold on to.

Sprout

Growth is learning to be accountable
especially for your own actions.

You've let other people
get in the way
of your goals
and
you damn sure didn't like it.

So why make allowances for yourself?
you still didn't like it.

You can do better than that,
treat yourself better than that.

No Shame

Are you happy with every action
you've ever done?
Every single one?

If you tell me 'yes'
I'll know you're lying.
You've found some of those things horrifying.

A piece,
a memory,
a sharp ass fragment
that you've secretly wished
would stop hindering your shift to an altruist.

A thought,
an ideology,
an outlook
you're ashamed of.

A perverse fucked up puppy love,
an action,
a word

or phrase
that had you in constant self-praise.

Are you happy with how
you've interacted with everyone?
If you tell me 'yes'
I'll know what you've done.

The lack of accountability
being the scariest one.

Truth

What's the worst that could happen
if everyone saw the real you?
You'd be so free:
Everyone would either love you
or
let you be.

Cycles

I've always been told
I had an old soul,
but maybe my soul is just exhausted.

Career Path

Struggling with finding my place,
figuring out what's right for me
and
realizing what's wrong.
Do you understand how damaging
it is to be constantly told your path isn't right?
Your career isn't worthwhile?

"You need to think more seriously
about your future!"

Do you not think that's what I'm doing?
I'm figuring it out
and
that's all you've got to offer me?

Tired

I'm tired

of making the best
out of shitty situations,
why must I have to?
I'd much rather
be happy
and
struggle to make my dreams
come true
rather than
making money
and
being miserable.

of seeing a part of myself die
every morning
in the mirror,
as I get ready
to go to a job I truly despise.

Questioning

I don't understand the point of life
if it's only going to involve
doing things I don't want to do.

Why must I be unhappy to live?
What sense does that make?
I want a life full of fun opportunities,
wild adventures,
and
undeniable belief.

I want a life worth living:
not a miserable existence,
constantly doing things I don't want to do.

Untitled

I have never wanted something
as bad as I want total freedom:
from work,
from self-doubt
from insecurity.

When I realize that I cannot have it
I want it even more.

Overthinking

Reduced to finding comfort
locked in the depths of my brain
where only I can control
what can hurt me
and what cannot

(right?)

Heads or Tails

I am but a simple fool
content in my scholar costume
or
was it
I am a content scholar
in a simple fool's outfit?

Whose asking?

Hubris and the Fall

Icarus and I
have a lot in common:
eyes constantly fixed
with no understanding
of the dangers in never looking away

But because He and I
have borrowed freedoms,
we understand the beauty
found in the pain of loss:

It feels like the blistering of skin
with your nerves on fire,
a heat rash of amazement over exposed faces.
Hair standing on end,
before the fall into contented bliss –
like feeling cold air kisses
and
soothed overheated flesh.

Our eyes still pinned
to the prizes we will never claim:

He, with an unquenchable thirst
for his own freedom.
Fingers stretched towards the sun
and
counting down the seconds
till he touched it,
wax wings shedding teardrops in their wake
–
And I, gasping for air
lungs feeling full of water,
eyes steadily trained on the ground beneath my feet,
too afraid of being blinded
to even know how to reach.

He was finally free enough to touch the sun
and
I was learning what it meant to want –
but his borrowed wings couldn't carry him
and
my anxiety wraps claws around my neck.

Icarus and I
have a lot in common,
he just flew too high
and
I was swiftly pulled under.

Tongue Tied

Sometimes It's hard for me to articulate
what's bouncing around in my head:
strong emotions strangle my words,
leaving me flustered and isolated –
unable to communicate my desires,
my dreams,
my wishes.

Who knew how difficult it would be for me
to make my own mouth work
while my brain runs a mile a minute?

Noise

Every time I get excited to show
the world what I made
here comes anxiety
loud and proud:

Roaring "it's just like everything else,"
and
screeching "it's nothing special!"
So instant it's overwhelming.
So obnoxious it's nauseating.
So loud it must be right.

Now so quiet it has become right
(but only because you listened to it).

Garden

Carefully watering my emotions,
my flowerbeds each in different stages:

Anger is overgrown wildflowers in shades
of reds and oranges –
Happiness is a plot full of Sunflowers
with their faces pointed towards the sky
and
my sadness,
a low-down sea of teal and white:
mistaken for weeds
yet never neglected.
Disappointment paints some petals purple
and
pink blossoms where there is love –

A healthy garden
is a colorful one.

Creation

Mold yourself
into the person you'd love –
you're always going to
put up with you.

Let's make this an enjoyable life.

Joy's Thief

To say I don't compare myself
to anyone else
would be to lie –

All I can do is remind myself that
I'm going the right speed
in the right direction.

If I told myself anything else
I would have lost everything I gained.

Confidence

Don't walk towards your goals-
run for your dreams!
Yet you won't.

How about you tell me everything
you have to lose
and
I'll tell you everything you have to gain.

Don't worry –
my answer will always
be more thought out than yours.

Sugar Rush

Can't you taste it?

Your dreams:
super sweet
and
within your grasp.

I'd bet they'd make your hands sticky.

Your candy-coated moment is coming.

Black Girl Joy

A small, sweet sound
bubbled up out of my mouth,
squeezing past my lips
to startle me:

Laughter,

I had forgotten what happiness tasted like.

A fight between the Brain and the Heart

One sinks its teeth in to be heard
whereas
one sinks its claws in to be understood.

No Mistakes Were Made

Accept yourself in
whatever
and
all the ways
your body tells you.
In all the ways your eyes see you.
In every way your heart expresses.

A love story between the heart and the cage that contains it

My heart beats against my ribs
pressing kisses to bone twigs
loving touches in rhythmic pattern
comparing my ribs to rings around Saturn.

This loving tale forages on strongly
making my body's third-wheeling a hobby,
My lungs realize they stand no chance
for claiming the ribs attention
was the heart.

Simply smitten the bones made space
to help the heart keep its steady pace
a protective stance it's taken in
keeping its treasure safe within.

What It Will Cost You

Whenever you end up doubting yourself
ask yourself this:
"What have I got to lose?"

I bet you've already lost 'everything' once before
I bet you'll lose 'everything' once more.

So, lose it,
then wait and see.
You'll find something else
worth 'everything' to you.
Trust me.

Subjective

How one woman cherishes a Rose,
another does a Common daisy.
A Chrysanthemum.
A Tiger lily.
Forget-me-nots.

How one-man paints nothing but Dahlias
another sings of Sunflowers...
or was it Buttercups?
Magnolias?
Blue orchids?

Ask any of these flower people
what they love the most:
"Their petals,
their colors,
their shapes and their sizes!"

How hardy or delicate,
how difficult or simple.
How different.
How they exist only for themselves –

for their own survival alone.

See yourself how you'd see flowers:
gorgeously diverse
and
distinctively beautiful.

Dwight

My love,
I get from my father –
it's selfless:
ask for a sliver
and
he'll hand over the whole.

I learned this love from him –
my father
with a funny personality:
unique
and
unapologetic.

My love,
was handed down by my father –
playfully crafted
with roller-coaster rides
and
blueberry muffins.

My,
this,
love is selfless.

Wendy

My love,
I get from my mother –
it's confident:
"You can turn to me
and
I'll always be there."
I learned this love from her –
my mother
with her strengths:
warm hugs
and
quick wit.
My love,
was passed down from my mother –
admiringly shaped
with amused acceptance
and
nuanced gifts.
My,
this,
love is confident.

Another Year

Why does it seem
that the older I get
the less desirable I'm made to be?

As if my age and experience
are hinderances
and the only
sensible quality
a woman can offer
is youth.

I am so much more than my age.

Taste Test

I refuse to do anything in halves.
I will not make myself smaller,
easier to swallow,
safer to digest:

I will never shrink my feelings.
I am an all or nothing type of experience
either accept that or choke.

Dead End

No one
is entitled to me in any form
that I am not willing to give.

I will not repeat myself.

Perception

I am complex and multifaceted,
I am an amalgamation of many wonderful traits,
of many ideals,
but what I am not
is patient

enough to explain myself to you

If you can't look at me
and see my complexity,
my value,
than you ignorantly aren't looking.

I will not waste my time
explaining my heart to you.

Head Start

What do I have to prove?
Well, that's between me,
myself,
and
I.

The only competition I have
is with myself,
for myself,
about myself.

I don't have anything to prove to you.

Quality

I wonder if me praising my blackness,
loving on my blackness,
is making you uncomfortable?

If it is let me ask you this:
how may I love myself
if I cannot love such a defining feature of mine?
Is it not a part of me?
Does it not partially define me?

How may I love myself,
If I cannot appreciate my blackness?
My heritage?
My culture?
My essence?

If my love letters to my blackness
make you uncomfortable:

I am not the problem.

Enthusiast

If I'm going to scar
let them be beautiful
and
of my own design.

Why allow others
to scar you for free
when tattoos exist?

I'd much rather be a human canvas
than a
human dartboard.

From Infinity to Infinity

I will always stand with the women
who look like me first.
The women
with broad and prominent noses –
the kind of noses as wide,
as wild,
and as beautiful
as every region of Africa.

The women whose skin is only as rich as this Earth:
the darkest and most understated
color of life.
The most diverse in its shades.

I will always stand with the women
whose eyes are the color of earthquakes
and
sandstorms –
The color of indignant fury
and

forcibly suppressed self-expression.

The women
who aren't allowed to laugh loudly,
complain,
get frustrated
or
be themselves.

The women
who've only ever been given
'struggle love' narratives
and
labeled uneducated
or
told they speak white.

I will always stand for the women
who've risked it all so that my hair
can coil,
spiral
and
stretch in whatever direction it wanted –
in any place it wanted.

I will always stand with women
with experiences like mine.
I see them
and
I think they're beautiful –
which in turn means I'm beautiful,
strong,

and
worth so much more than society says
I am
Just like them.
So, I'll stand for them first.
Always.
Forever.

Midas

My hands,
in all their blackness,
are magic!

So, why wouldn't I want to
support hands that look just like mine,
minds that think similarly to mine,
ears that have heard the same sounds as mine,
eyes that have witnessed the same things as mine?

Why wouldn't I want to support
these equally magical people of mine?
Everything they,
and myself,
touch
turns to gold.

How beautiful.

Titan

I am not Atlas,
for the world is not my burden
nor should it set on my shoulders,
yet here is where it's set
because I am a black woman
and
apparently the center of all your problems,
so, you set the world on my shoulders
and
am outraged when I drop it.

You forget that I am not Atlas,
and
your problems are not my burden.

Encompassing

When you love yourself
you'll see that same love spilling
everywhere else.
Into everything else.

You'll watch that love shine on everyone around you –
Raining complimenting kisses
and
whispering praises.
When you love yourself,
you'll see that same love reflected –
By similar people
who aren't emotionally draining.
Aren't emotionally taxing.
Aren't demanding in any form.

Love yourself and
you'll surround yourself with
people who love themselves.
It'll make ya'll love each other more:
no competition.

They aren't you
and
you aren't them.
How perfect is that?
Knowing that you both are
exactly who you're supposed to be,
That you're both valuable.

When you love yourself,
you realize you can do anything
and
the right people will be standing there
helping you,
guiding you,
and
cheering for you.

Love yourself
and
you'll find yourself cheering for them too.
How perfect is that?

PLATONIC

When It Rains

I always watched it happen –
quick as lightening
and
right before my eyes.

The silence was loud:
anyone could take my place.
I guess all you need
is to feel something-
whether that's at the cost
of your mental health
or
your friendships.

When it rains,
it pours,
right over that scorched patch:
our bond,
in the middle of our childhood lawn,
where all the toys are rusted.
The old footprints on the porch
further prove,

that I'm holding onto a ghost
solidified by my longing.

I thought the rain was peaceful.
Then came the thunder,
and I thought of the times you exploded-
A startling display of emotion
and
the flashes I glimpsed from the lightning strike
illuminated the real you.

I guess when it rains,
it pours
and
all I can do
is watch the flood
sweep everything you've become down the street.

Not Enough

I love you
but that doesn't mean
I have to
be with you.

I love you
but that doesn't mean
I need to
tolerate you.

I love you
and yet I can
still see when you
simply aren't good for me.

I love you
but that doesn't mean
you can stay.

So, what if I love you?
Loving you isn't enough.

Goodbye

We might not have been close
yet you floated through my life
like a ghost –
a whisper here,
a note left there.

Your presence was felt everywhere
so, tell me why does it hurt
after watching this friendship burst?
Space from her was truly overdue,
but why did you have to
get rid of me too?

You didn't have to push me to the curb,
but I can't fault you
for doing what's best for you.

Them

I prided myself

in never needing anyone,

yet somehow
found myself surrounded by
irreplaceable people.

Passage

Do not think
that I am ungrateful
for
every second,
every minute,
every hour,
every day,
every week,
every month
and
every year
that they still choose
to be a part of my life:

These special people of mine.

Pieces

I hate puzzles,
but you already knew that.
I found it exhausting sorting through every piece
until I realized
It's like putting you and I together –
I searched for you
and
had never been so happy as when I found you.
We fit,
our ideals seamlessly bled together
and
our fashion might contrast,
but it makes for a beautiful picture.

I still hate puzzles
but
now the searching makes sense.

The perfect fit
is worth all the time it took.

Silver

It hurts
when I'm handing out first-place medals
and
receive second-place medals in return:

It hurts when society deems
only romantic love worthy of a first-place medal
and
your friendships agree.

23

Do you remember
the time spent in my parents' kitchen making eggs,
like I'm doing now and
sharing all of your worries with me?

The heavy secret you'd hidden
from even your parents,
you spilled to me,
over the sound of eggs sizzling.
Over the sound of your breath hitching.

Do you remember
the time spent in my parents' kitchen
where we talked about everything?

I wonder if you remember me the way I remember you.

I'm happy for where you ended up,
but I wish we still talked
like we did in my parents' kitchen
over the sound of eggs
cooking on the stove.

Loud & Proud

Here I am,

standing front and center
screaming at the top of my lungs:
"You've got this!"

"You're made for this!"

"There isn't anything you can't do!"

Here I am,

standing front and center
screaming at the top of my lungs:
"You're going to make it!"

I'm your biggest fan
and
I won't let you forget it.

Understanding

"Why poetry?"
she asks
and
all I could think to say was:
"Because it's the only way
my brain knows how to share
what it's really thinking."

I wish I had said:
"It's the only life raft left
that can connect my mouth –
my salvation –
to these drowning thoughts."

Her smile told me
she heard me loud
and
clear.

I'll always try to be better when it comes to you

I've noticed that within this friendship
I'm trying harder to be more like you
while you're trying to be more like me:

I love that you admire me
in the same ways that
I admire you.

We're so different,
you and I,
yet so similar.

Maybe that's why we work so well.
Maybe that's why we do better together.

Platonic Soulmate

I still sing songs
and
think about you:
kind of like
cheesy 90s RnB
while trying not to lose my cool –
It's not that
I'm feeling Romantic but romantic.

I love you
and
appreciate everything you do.

Pink + Green

You're sweet like spring strawberries
and
I'm tart like rhubarb –
Funny how we swapped colors,
my favorite summer child:
please continue
to lighten up my life.

The One

You,
to me,
are the warmest sweater I own.

You know,
the one that feels
like it's hugging me
every time I put it on
and
although it's a little tattered
it's still my favorite cold weather accessory.

It's soft from constant wear,
perfectly molded to keep me comfortable
and
effortlessly cute.

You know the sweater:

The one with the buttons the same color
as your chipped nail polish –
If I look closely enough my hair is there

woven into the soft fabric,
trying to curl into it,
like I curl into you.

You,
to me,
are the oldest sweater I own:
endlessly loved
and
always reliable –
You know the one.

Goals

There is no comparison
between you and me.

You're the reason I work so hard:
on my communication,
on hard conversations
and
most importantly on myself.

I want to be someone you're proud of,
because you're already that someone to me.

The Beginning

He only loved me as a friend
and
that was all the love I thought I needed:

Until you.

ROMANTIC

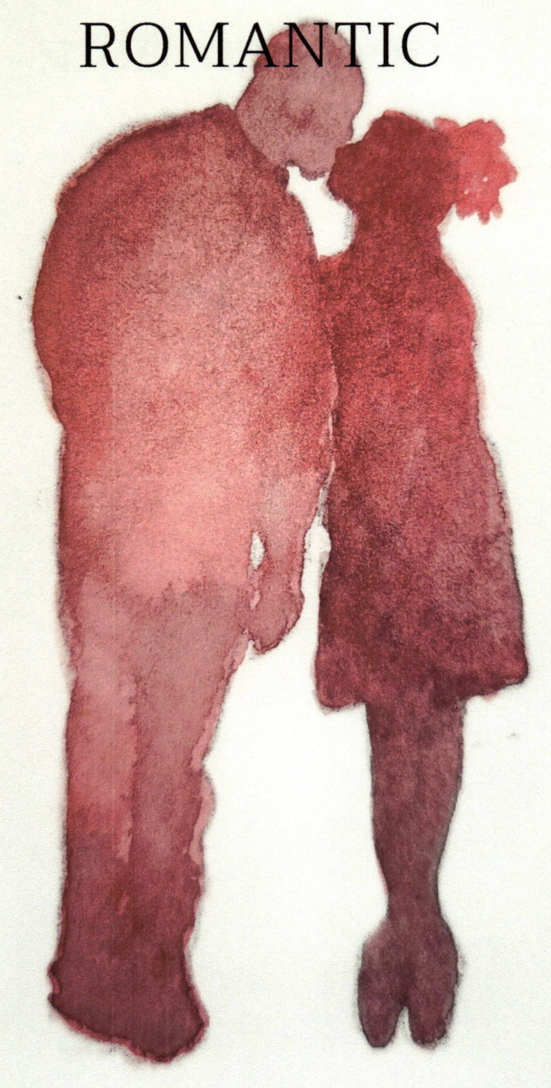

Treasure

Adventure –
What makes the heart pound?
I didn't want this,
But I did...
didn't I?

Exploration –
What she did with her mouth,
her fingers.
A controlling presence.

Conquest –
X marked the spot
or triangle
between my legs.

Self-Hatred part two

Up above:
sweating, straining, grunting.
The knowledge of a glide between my legs,
my body knowing what to do.
Blank eyes: no sound.

I should be feeling something.
My mind cannot process,

A shudder and done,
"Was that as good for you,
As it was for me?"

A feeling of disgust,
self-loathing.
I wanted to hate myself more:
so, I smiled.

Stages

I always find myself
having permanent conversations
with temporary people.

Negativity

You could never tell me what was wrong
so, I told myself.

Tears

My heart still cries for yours,

no matter how much I beg and plead
for it to hush.

No matter how much
I try to remind it that you fumbled it,
that you attempted to break it.

My heart still cries for you

and I can't seem
to get it to stop.

Throw Away

You loved me
and then you didn't.

I just couldn't understand
how easily you could misplace
my love for you.

How quickly you forgot your love for me.

I just couldn't understand...
Was it something I did?
Was it something I said?
Was it even me
(or you)?

Romance

When I read,
I like to fill my life
with whatever I'm missing.

When I was with you,
I didn't touch horror –
My life was scary enough.

When I was with you,
I didn't need mysteries –
You left me with enough.

But romance,
that's all I read
because within our relationship
that was the only thing missing.

Eden

Heaven was between my arms
and
pillowed amongst my breasts.

You claimed paradise was leaking
from between my thighs
yet you left.

I bet you think
you're someplace better now.

Good for you.

Neglect

You are not allowed to use me
to sate your needs
while mine remain

STARVED

What a waste

I'm not even surprised anymore
when I tap on your promises
and
they chime like crystal.

How pretty they are
catching dust on display.

Completely empty.

No Better

Sick with the knowledge that
I want to hurt you
like you hurt me.

And here I thought
I was better than you.

Black Widow

Sitting in the middle of my web
watching your big lies,
stick to silvery silk ties
nothing more than fat flies.

A hunger to consume taking over –
It's not the bugs that I want,
It's your head on a platter.
I'm constantly dreaming of the blood splatter
but what's it matter?
My affection left you flattered.

So, step into my nest
and
I'll happily get rid of one more pest.

Congratulations

You've finally managed to do it:
you've killed the cat,
you've killed the dog
and
you've killed me.

We're dead to you,

Just like you are to us.
Just like I've killed you.

Halos & Horns

Oh my,
is that an Angel I spy,
amongst the Devils that I identify?
Singing praises at my feet,
oh, how their devotion to me is semi-sweet.

Why would none just take my hand?
Was this some unspoken no man's land?
Yet they keep singing at my feet,
reminding me devotion is bitter-sweet.

What Are Butterflies?

These feelings
coil and wind themselves around
and
around
within my stomach,
flashing smooth iridescent scales
and
venom spitting fangs.
Surprisingly warm,
but
one wrong move
and
the bite –
these feelings –
could kill me.

“I want you, but I can’t love you”

It was expected
but still hurt to
hear you admit that
I wasn’t worth the effort to you.

Saints

Falling in love with every man
that comes begging for asylum in my church
and
every woman that uses her mouth
to knock at my temple doors -
with the words of praise they press into my flesh.

I love being worshipped like a goddess
but
I also wish to be loved like one.

Please just look at me

I just
want to be looked at
like I mean something
to you.

By you.

Only you.

Want me too

A billion thoughts
and
they're all simply just of you.

Please tell me,
do you think of me too...?

Please,
even if it's once a day,
think of me
with ease.

Flood Warning

Will the changing of my seasons
have you relocating:
somewhere it's always sunny
or
preparing for the Monsoon
and
welcoming the flood of my emotions?

Please stay:
So, I may water you
with the thunderstorms my eyes shed,
So, I can dry you with my sun scorched kisses
So, I may support your growth with a tight embrace.

I'll flood you,
but only in love
and
only if you let me.

Please stay.

Breaking my own heart

Why do I constantly
tell myself the worst?

As if someone couldn't love me
the way that I am,
with no complaints.

The Color Purple

To avoid a singular color
I've started to interview –
my head
against my heart
against you.

My brain refuses to let me cry
and
my heart refuses to feel inferior
while I
refuse to be hurt again.

By you.
By anyone.
Ever again.
Never again.

Dominance

Submission isn't hard,
especially when there's trust –
Much like how a dog rolls over
and
shows you the most vulnerable spot on their body
I must see a give
and
take
before raising my chin and exposing my throat –
I can lose a lot more
than just my pride if I yield to you.

Show me how much you deserve it.
Show me how you'll earn it.

Speaks for Itself

I refuse to chase anyone,
I shouldn't have to –
If you want a place within my life,
I shouldn't have to pull teeth
to have you tell me so.

Passion

Looking at you makes my heart glow bright,
sending out flashes of pure fire light.
Making me glow concerningly hot,
my tongue melting into one big knot –
Gorgeous, you got me burning up,
watching as my heart erupts,
baby will these feelings spread?

I want to stay your girl,
bathed in red.

Mirror

I envy the way
you press your lips against mine –
So soft
and
sure
while mine tremble
and
tense.
A million thoughts flooding my mind:
"Am I doing this right?"
"Does my breath stink?"
"Are my lips soft enough?"

But they dance right back out
when your lips flutter over mine
and
they tremble
and
tense.
"I like the way you kiss me."
It shows me you care.

Territory

Tried to explain
how I woke up
wanting to confirm you're mine,
but I couldn't explain it right
so,
I settled on:

"I woke up wanting to kiss you."

"Two people who cannot understand each other"

She spoke in colorful phrases:
her love tinted pink,
her anger bathed in reds
and
her sadness a deep purple:
as expansive as space.
She hummed in pastels
and
cursed
and
complained in fluorescent hues:
bright
bold
and
entirely unapologetic.
Her life was luminous and busy
but a gray scale of a man is what caught her attention.
He was a thunderstorm full

of bright flashes of animation
that danced quicker than lightening
across his face
and
sent a current through her blood.
    She couldn't understand the relaxed,
muted greys of his calm demeaner
or the never ending
and
utterly impenetrable black void that is his depression.
    His anxieties a blank white against
her color-wheel.
Where she speeds through every color imaginable
in a matter of seconds,
he was a steady
and
stable
dove grey.
Reliable,
dependable,
if not a bit boring.
Even though she expressed herself
in rainbow traces
and
he merely lingered in monochromatic shades.
    They learned to appreciate
the variation:
even if they couldn't understand it.

Love's Season

Are you surprised?
Well spring came over me:

The season of
love
and
sex
always turns me into a mess.

I just couldn't get my thoughts
off your hands on my things –
pushing them high
before
spreading them wide

I've become excited
for this very
'you' specific ride.

Listen

I cannot help but think of you:
your hands around my neck,
pointer finger shoved into my mouth.
Panting, shuddering.
Actual feeling.

A light being lit inside of my chest.
"Harder," I whisper,
the careful way you do as I ask –

Always paying attention to me
what a feeling,
an actual feeling.

Sex isn't just an act with you,
it's a beautiful feeling.

2016

Laying in bed I can feel your finger tracing:
my lines,
jagged edges and soft spots.

Your lips feathering kisses from:
my sleep laden eyes
to my jaw and back.

Eyes, jaw and back.
Eyes, jaw and back.

My back arches.
Reaching out,
fingers splayed wide –
fanning through open air
eyes flying open:
nothing.

Sitting up disorientated I realize:
you're out of my reach for a while.

sigh.

You laugh into my neck,
kissing it.

"I miss you too."

Back to bed with your fingers tracing:
my lines,
jagged edges and soft spots.

Muse

He makes me feel like a painting
done by Picasso or Michael Angelo
and
far prettier than the Mona Lisa,
A Madonna and child the world has never seen.

I love that he turned his heart into a museum,
to proudly display
the art that is me.

All Mine

I don't ever want anyone
to view you the way I do:
the purest girl in the room
that I can't help but want to consume.

Love Letter

I'll write about you
because that's what I do:
record your smile
and
your laugh
in sun bright imagery
simply because that's how I see it.

I'll write about my love for you
because it's what I should do.

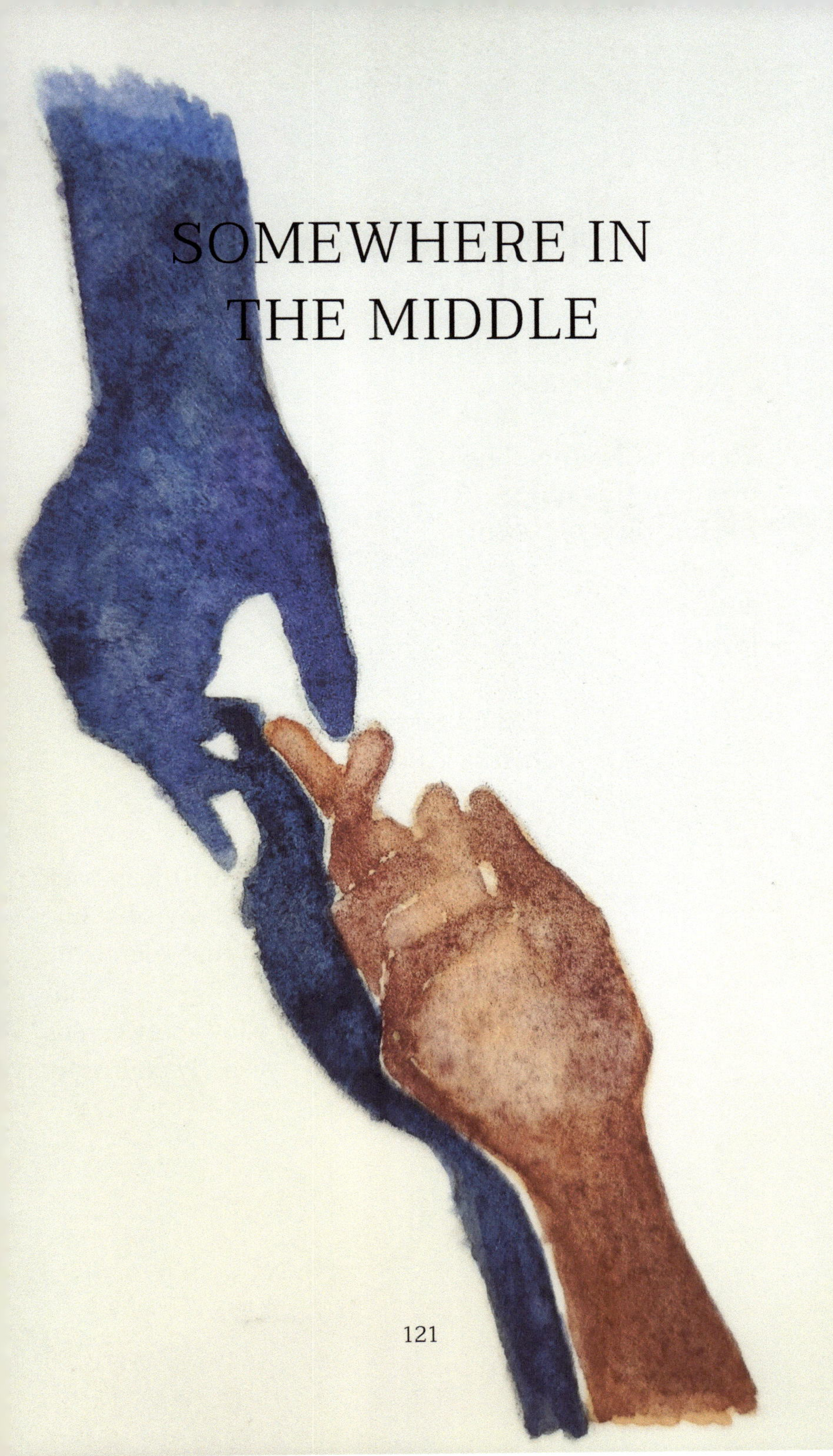

SOMEWHERE IN THE MIDDLE

Puppy Love

Youth had us fumbling
over that thin line –
the one right between
friends
and
lovers.

The initial taste savory
before losing its flavor

A swift leap back
over that invisible line
preserved that friendship
but
left the love between us
sweetly confused.

I Wish We Could Be More

Sometimes,
I look at you
and my heart

stutters,
stumbles,
and trips

right on over itself.
I can't help that:

I love you

as more than a friend.
I can't help that:

I know we're better off,
right where we are –
As friends.
Only friends.

My favorite star

I've always wondered:
are the stars salty
like my tears?

They must cry
being so far
from everyone
and
everything
while
being viewed from a distance
that only measures
in long lost time:
no care in how they're fairing.

I've always wondered:
are the stars salty
like my tears?

They must cry
when they burn everything
they love

and
cherish.
Never allowed to hold on too tightly
yet
too lonely to ever let them go.

I've always wondered:
are the stars salty
like my tears
because they're beautiful
and
out of reach.
Just like you.

When I think of you,
I think of the stars
and
my tears are salty.

Natural Disaster

I always circle you:
a personal moon
or maybe
you're a whirlpool
wishing to suck me in closer,
yet
unaware I'd drown
under the weight of this pining:
surrounding me in its cold loneliness
and
running over my head,
into my mouth
and
burning my nose.

I always circle you,
captured by your gaze's current –
My heart is spinning thinking about it,
you're so dangerous(ly beautiful).

I always circle you,
pulled in by your

soft heart:
the middle being the safest spot,
yet
the hardest to get to.

I always circle you,
hoping you'll drag me in
and
never push me back out.

If Only I Had the Courage

In my mind
The Sun rises with you:
he shines just for you!
He warms for your comfort,
just so you're happy.

I wish I could tell you that.
"What about the Moon?"
you'd ask.
and
if I had the courage
I'd tell you:

"We talk about your beauty."
How she can see the real you
and
"I bathe in the song she sings of you."
I soak in it –
I gulp it down like an addict,
obsessed with her honey coated honesty

about you:
your faults,
your weaknesses,
your secrets.
I swallow your melodies
and
your harmonies fill me up right.

I think about all the ways I would love you:
bathed in golden light
or
praised by Moon's sight.

Moon of My Life

Waxing your being with
twin compliments:

adoration
and
appreciation

just so your insecurities wane.

You look the prettiest in your full glory.

Practitioner

If I were religious
you'd be my religion:
your name my prayer,
your heartbeat would be gospel,
your smile the sermon –
worship would happen
every day of the week
and
you'd be observed 24/7.

I'll be your most devote follower,
please anoint me in your love.

Winners Circle

I would never treat you like a trophy
because I know how that feels,
but sometimes when I look at you
I get this yearning:

A feeling that leaves me lacking –
a pity that reminds me
of all the dreams I've pinned
to sports I'll never achieve.

My legs never carry me far enough,
my lungs never hold enough air,
and
my arms are always outstretched
hoping to close around that golden glint.
My prize.
What I worked so hard for:
You.

Too bad
I can never hold myself up
to the standards I set to deserve you.

Possessive

I can't stand the thought
of anyone taking you from me
so, I'll keep you all to myself
even if it means
keeping you locked in the depths of my being.

I want to be the only one
that can read every twitch of your lips
and
tell stories about every wrinkle around your eyes.

I want to be the one
that knows you the most.

I want to be the one that understands you.

Scaredy Cat

It's a little alarming
that I find cutting myself open
and
spattering my heart on the pages
for strangers to see
so much easier
than
trying to tell you how I feel.

I find I'd rather be rejected by millions
than by you.

The End

I craft this story,
just for you:
letter by letter,
every awkward pause by
tearstained exclamation –

I spill these feelings,
just for you:
shy smiles
and
strong hugs,
punctuated with nervous chatter –

I present this to you:
I hope you love it,
because I wrote it all about you.

www.ingramcontent.com/pod-product-compliance
Ingram Content Group UK Ltd.
Pitfield, Milton Keynes, MK11 3LW, UK
UKHW060359300726
14090UKWH00001B/20

* 9 7 9 8 2 1 8 1 6 6 3 3 5 *